THE
POLISH
AMERICANS

THE
POLISH
AMERICANS

Rachel Toor

CHELSEA HOUSE PUBLISHERS

New York   Philadelphia

Cover Photo: Polish-American World War I volunteers gathered outside a Pennsylvania confectionery wield a sign that says in English, "Good-bye America, we go to struggle with the desperate Kaiser for your freedom and ours."

Chelsea House Publishers

Editor-in-Chief: Nancy Toff
Executive Editor: Remmel T. Nunn
Managing Editor: Karyn Gullen Browne
Copy Chief: Juliann Barbato
Picture Editor: Adrian G. Allen
Art Director: Giannella Garrett
Manufacturing Manager: Gerald Levine

The Peoples of North America

Senior Editor: Sam Tanenhaus

Staff for THE POLISH AMERICANS

Assistant Editor: Abigail Meisel
Copy Editor: Terrance Dolan
Deputy Copy Chief: Ellen Scordato
Editorial Assistant: Theodore Keyes
Picture Research: PAR/NYC
Designer: Noreen M. Lamb
Layout: Louise Lippin
Production Coordinator: Joseph Romano
Cover Illustration: Paul Biniasz
Banner Design: Hrana L. Janto

3 5 7 9 8 6 4 2

Library of Congress Cataloging in Publication Data

Toor, Rachel.
  Polish Americans.

  (The Peoples of North America)
  Bibliography: p.
  Includes index.
  Summary: Discusses the history, culture, and religion of the Poles, factors encouraging their emigration, and their acceptance as an ethnic group in North America.
  1. Polish Americans—Juvenile literature.
[1. Polish Americans] I. Title. II. Series.
E184.P7T57 1988   973'.049185   87-26818
ISBN 0-87754-895-1
      0-7910-0274-8 (pbk.)

Contents

THE PEOPLES OF NORTH AMERICA

CHELSEA HOUSE PUBLISHERS

A
NATION
OF
NATIONS

Daniel Patrick Moynihan

The Constitution of the United States begins: "We the People of the United States . . ." Yet, as we know, the United States is not made up of a single group of people. It is made up of many peoples. Immigrants from Europe, Asia, Africa, and Central and South America settled in North America seeking a new life filled with opportunities unavailable in their homeland. Coming from many nations, they forged one nation and made it their own. More than 100 years ago, Walt Whitman expressed this perception of America as a melting pot: "Here is not merely a nation, but a teeming Nation of nations."

Although the ingenuity and acts of courage of these immigrants, our ancestors, shaped the North American way of life, we sometimes take their contributions for granted. This fine series, *The Peoples of North America*, examines the experiences and contributions of the immigrants and how these contributions determined the future of the United States and Canada.

Immigrants did not abandon their ethnic traditions when they reached the shores of North America. Each ethnic group had its own customs and traditions, and each brought different experiences, accomplishments, skills, values, styles of dress, and tastes in food that lingered long after its arrival. Yet this profusion of differences created a singularity, or bond, among the immigrants.

The United States and Canada are unusual in this respect. Whereas religious and ethnic differences have sparked intolerance throughout the rest of the world—from the 17th-century religious wars to the 19th-century nationalist movements in Europe to the near extermination of the Jewish people under Nazi Germany— North Americans have struggled to learn how to respect each other's differences and live in harmony.

Millions of immigrants from scores of homelands brought diversity to our continent. In a mass migration, some 12 million immigrants passed through the waiting rooms of New York's Ellis Island; thousands more came to the West Coast. At first, these immigrants were welcomed because labor was needed to meet the demands of the Industrial Age. Soon, however, the new immigrants faced the prejudice of earlier immigrants who saw them as a burden on the economy. Legislation was passed to limit immigration. The Chinese Exclusion Act of 1882 was among the first laws closing the doors to the promise of America. The Japanese were also effectively excluded by this law. In 1924, Congress set immigration quotas on a country-by-country basis.

Such prejudices might have triggered war, as they did in Europe, but North Americans chose negotiation and compromise, instead. This determination to resolve differences peacefully has been the hallmark of the peoples of North America.

The remarkable ability of Americans to live together as one people was seriously threatened by the issue of slavery. It was a symptom of growing intolerance in the world. Thousands of settlers from the British Isles had arrived in the colonies as indentured servants, agreeing to work for a specified number of years on farms or as apprentices in return for passage to America and room and board. When the first Africans arrived in the then-British colonies during the 17th century, some colonists thought that they too should be treated as indentured servants. Eventually, the question of whether the Africans should be viewed as indentured, like the English, or as slaves who could be owned for life, was considered in a Maryland court. The court's calamitous decree held that blacks were slaves bound to lifelong servitude, and so were their children.

America went through a time of moral examination and civil war before it finally freed African slaves and their descendants. The principle that all people are created equal had faced its greatest challenge and survived.

Yet the court ruling that set blacks apart from other races fanned flames of discrimination that burned long after slavery was abolished—and that still flicker today. The concept of racism had existed for centuries in countries throughout the world. For instance, when the Manchus conquered China in the 13th century, they decreed that Chinese and Manchus could not intermarry. To impress their superiority on the conquered Chinese, the Manchus ordered all Chinese men to wear their hair in a long braid called a queue.

By the 19th century, some intellectuals took up the banner of racism, citing Charles Darwin. Darwin's scientific studies hypothesized that highly evolved animals were dominant over other animals. Some advocates of this theory applied it to humans, asserting that certain races were more highly evolved than others and thus were superior.

This philosophy served as the basis for a new form of discrimination, not only against nonwhite people but also against various ethnic groups. Asians faced harsh discrimination and were depicted by popular 19th-century newspaper cartoonists as depraved, degenerate, and deficient in intelligence. When the Irish flooded American cities to escape the famine in Ireland, the cartoonists caricatured the typical "Paddy" (a common term for Irish immigrants) as an apelike creature with jutting jaw and sloping forehead.

By the 20th century, racism and ethnic prejudice had given rise to virulent theories of a Northern European master race. When Adolf Hitler came to power in Germany in 1933, he popularized the notion of Aryan supremacy. "Aryan," a term referring to the Indo-European races, was applied to so-called superior physical characteristics such as blond hair, blue eyes, and delicate facial features. Anyone with darker and heavier features was considered inferior. Buttressed by these theories, the German Nazi state from

1933 to 1945 set out to destroy European Jews, along with Poles, Russians, and other groups considered inferior. It nearly succeeded. Millions of these people were exterminated.

The tragedies brought on by ethnic and racial intolerance throughout the world demonstrate the importance of North America's efforts to create a society free of prejudice and inequality.

A relatively recent example of the New World's desire to resolve ethnic friction nonviolently is the solution the Canadians found to a conflict between two ethnic groups. A long-standing dispute as to whether Canadian culture was properly English or French resurfaced in the mid-1960s, dividing the peoples of the French-speaking Quebec Province from those of the English-speaking provinces. Relations grew tense, then bitter, then violent. The Royal Commission on Bilingualism and Biculturalism was established to study the growing crisis and to propose measures to ease the tensions. As a result of the commission's recommendations, all official documents and statements from the national government's capital at Ottawa are now issued in both French and English, and bilingual education is encouraged.

The year 1980 marked a coming of age for the United States's ethnic heritage. For the first time, the U.S. Census asked people about their ethnic background. Americans chose from more than 100 groups, including French Basque, Spanish Basque, French Canadian, Afro-American, Peruvian, Armenian, Chinese, and Japanese. The ethnic group with the largest response was English (49.6 million). More than 100 million Americans claimed ancestors from the British Isles, which includes England, Ireland, Wales, and Scotland. There were almost as many Germans (49.2 million) as English. The Irish-American population (40.2 million) was third, but the next largest ethnic group, the Afro-Americans, was a distant fourth (21 million). There was a sizable group of French ancestry (13 million), as well as of Italian (12 million). Poles, Dutch, Swedes, Norwegians, and Russians followed. These groups, and other smaller ones, represent the wondrous profusion of ethnic influences in North America.

Canada, too, has learned more about the diversity of its population. Studies conducted during the French/English conflict showed that Canadians were descended from Ukrainians, Germans, Italians, Chinese, Japanese, native Indians, and Eskimos, among others. Canada found it had no ethnic majority, although nearly half of its immigrant population had come from the British Isles. Canada, like the United States, is a land of immigrants for whom mutual tolerance is a matter of reason as well as principle.

The people of North America are the descendants of one of the greatest migrations in history. And that migration is not over. Koreans, Vietnamese, Nicaraguans, Cubans, and many others are heading for the shores of North America in large numbers. This mix of cultures shapes every aspect of our lives. To understand ourselves, we must know something about our diverse ethnic ancestry. Nothing so defines the North American nations as the motto on the Great Seal of the United States: *E Pluribus Unum*—Out of Many, One. ∾

On the Fourth of July, Polish Americans pose with their homemade float on Main Street in Nanticoke, Pennsylvania.

FROM POLAND TO POLONIA

Once I thought to write a history of the immigrants in America. Then I discovered that the immigrants were American history.

—Oscar Handlin

Immigrants from Poland have been living in the United States for a long time—since before the loose confederation of English colonies formally joined together to form a single political entity in the 18th century. The great Polish migration occurred in the 19th and early 20th centuries, when more than 2.5 million Poles reached American shores. Today, the 8 million people in the United States who claim Polish ancestry represent one of the nation's largest ethnic groups. They came, they created a new world for themselves, and they thrived. In their homeland, many had been peasant farmers, near the bottom of the socioeconomic ladder. From humble beginnings they moved into American communities and created what came to be known as *Polonia*, Latin for Poland.

A Polish immigrant stands dressed in Old World garb, c. 1900.

The Dream of America

Unlike two other ethnic groups who struggled to better their lot in the United States in the late 19th century—blacks who were trying to shake off the yoke of slavery and Asians who came to the West Coast looking for work—Poles physically blended in with Caucasian Americans of long standing. But adjusting to American society posed problems. Polish immigrants faced harsh prejudice when they searched for jobs and places to live. Unskilled, they were channeled into industries that exploited their strong bodies and eagerness to succeed. They worked seemingly endless hours in mills and mines, struggling to eke out a living. The stalwartness of Polish immigrants earned them a reputation that gradually hardened into a stereotype. In Pittsburgh, Poles were known for being virtuous, quiet, and hardworking. A Pittsburgh foreman said, "Give [them] rye bread, a herring, and a beer and they are all right." According to another stereotype, however, Poles should not be given too much beer: Their drinking was often thought to be uncontrollable.

Long before Polish immigrants came to America, the economy of their homeland had been in decline. The original immigrants did not intend to settle permanently in the New World but rather to make money to take home to Poland. It was not financial reasons alone, however, that led so many to make the hard decision to leave Poland. For as long as the country had been in economic decline, it had also suffered repeated intervention, subjugation, and oppression by foreign powers, having been divided and occupied for almost 1,000 years. Politically aware Poles felt the attraction of a brave new world, a place where citizens had managed to rebel against a tyrannical king and set up a system of government unlike any other; a place where people had fought for their independence and instituted a democracy to protect what they had gained. No im-

Poles, such as those pictured here in Mauch Chunk, Pennsylvania, in 1940, provided American steel and mining companies with a steady supply of labor.

migrant group appreciated America's democratic experiment more than the Poles.

They came, especially at the turn of the 20th century, in great numbers, and settled in large communities. Getting here was not easy, but their dreams spurred them on. In *Poland the Knight Among Nations*, published in 1907, Louis E. Van Norman wrote:

> While in Zbaráz [the province of Galicia] I visited a school for peasant children. Its sessions were held in a rustic little one-room building with the conventional thatched roof . . . . For my especial benefit, the prize scholar was asked where was America. He hesitated a moment, then he said he did not know, except that it was the country to which good Polish boys went when they died.

From Poland to Polonia

From thousands of miles away America did indeed seem a kind of heaven. But those who came first weathered a hellish ordeal. In addition to the discrimination they suffered from other Americans, Polish immigrants encountered tremendous obstacles on another important front: religion. Devoutly Catholic Poles found themselves in conflict with the Irish Catholics who monopolized the American Catholic church in the late 19th and early 20th centuries. Both groups belonged to the same faith, but within that faith many differences divided them: Poland and Ireland had their own national saints, their own traditional heritage, their own vision of the priesthood—in Poland, and later in Polonia, parish priests had almost unlimited control over the community. The Irish Americans resented the unique character of Polish Catholics, especially their unwillingness to use English as a language of worship. Gradually the Polish church gained acceptance worldwide, to the point where a Pole, Cardinal Karol Wojytla, became pope (John Paul II) in 1978.

The election of a Polish pope shows just how far these hardworking people have come. Individual Poles excel in the mainstream of American life—from politics to poetry, theater, film, music, and baseball. And as a

In 1974, parishioners of St. Valentine's Polish National Catholic Church receive Communion in Northampton, Massachusetts.

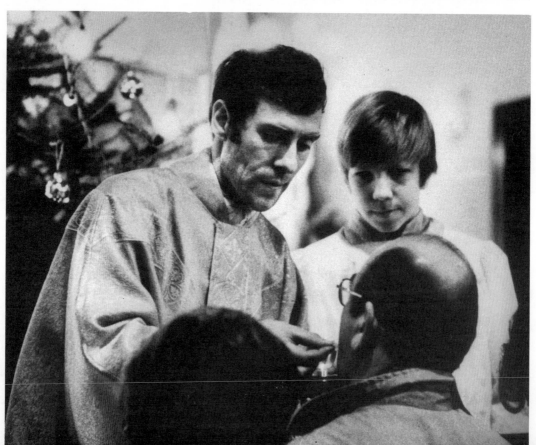

group, Polish Americans have gained considerable clout, a fact acknowledged by the nation's leaders. As former president Gerald Ford once remarked:

> It has been the policy of mine—and the policy of my Administration—to listen carefully to the voice of Polish America. When it comes to sacrifice and achievement, you have given more, far more than your share in making this the greatest country in the history of mankind.

Hundreds of thousands of Poles left tiny villages in the countryside and resettled in the crowded and confusing streets of New York City, Chicago, and other cities and towns in America. Leaving home was an act of faith, but as more immigrants sought prosperous shores across the Atlantic, Polish villages began to be dominated by the elderly, the ailing, and the young. It was hard for those who left, harder perhaps for those who stayed. But Polish immigrants in America did not forget, and what they saw as a moral obligation propelled them to keep up contacts with relatives and friends still in Poland and also with others who had made the long journey and had scattered across 3,000 miles of America. Because so many of the immigrants had similar backgrounds and experiences in the New World they felt encouraged to band together to ease the ordeal of readjustment. The large network of Polish Americans led one Greek immigrant to remark:

> We have been in America for six months . . . We have neither heard English nor become acquainted with Americans. In the mill there worked Polish men and women and only Polish was spoken in the factory and in the streets of the small town.

A Greek friend added, "I believe the captain of our ship made a mistake and instead of bringing us to America brought us to Poland." ∾

CRACOVIA.

RVDA FLVVIVS

An engraving details the Polish city of Kraków, located on the Vistula River.

THE PEOPLE OF THE FIELDS

Poland, a country in central Europe, borders on three other countries—East Germany to the west, Czechoslovakia to the south, and the Soviet Union to the east and northeast. Northwest lies the Baltic Sea, which provides access to the Atlantic Ocean. The total landmass of Poland roughly equals that of New Mexico, and about half the land is arable. Poland's inhabitants have traditionally been farmers, especially in the south, which boasts rich soil conducive to growing potatoes, beets, and grains such as wheat and barley. In recent decades, however, industry has begun to dominate the country's economy, and many goods pass through the shipyards of port cities on the Baltic coast. The largest of these cities, Gdańsk, drew worldwide attention in 1981. But that chapter occurs late in the nation's history and, like the story of Polish immigration, can only be understood in the light of much earlier events.

The House of Piast

According to legend, Polish history begins with Piast, a peasant boy who was told by two strangers that he would someday rule the land. Years later, Piast fulfilled this prophecy. The dynasty he launched ruled for 500 years and eventually united many of the scattered Slavonic tribes into a single Polish kingdom. Piast reigned over the extensive Polish plain, one of the main routes of entry for Europe's early migrants—Balts, Celts, Ger-

The bronze doors of Gniezno Cathedral, carved during the 12th century, depict St. Adalbert baptizing slaves who converted to Catholicism.

mans, Slavs, Huns, Scythians, Carpathians, and Mongols. The country now called Poland derived its name in the 10th century from Piast's tribe, the *Polonie* ("the people of the fields"), who settled on the banks of the river Warta, near present-day Poznań.

The official record of the House of Piast begins with the 10th-century A.D. prince, Mieszko I. The domain he ruled stretched from the Oder River (its western border) to the Vistula River (its eastern border). As the country grew, Mieszko held off the encroachment of Germanic tribes by allying with Bohemia, a secure region in nearby Czechoslovakia. The Bohemians were Christians and wanted Mieszko to join their faith. He complied and in 965 was baptized. He then dismissed his seven concubines, married a Bohemian princess, and placed his territory under the protection of the Roman Catholic church. Mieszko's successor, his son Boleslaw I, "the Brave," ruled from 992 to 1025. He expanded the country's borders as far south as the Carpathian Mountains and as far west as Pomerania and Moravia until Poland encompassed virtually the same territory established nearly 1,000 years later in the wake of World War II. Germanic tribes still threatened the nation, but Boleslaw's forces checked their advances.

When this splendid monarch died, however, Poland slipped into decline, and the country's next leaders were recognized only as dukes by central Europe's chief power, the Holy Roman Empire. Boleslaw III, "the Wry," who took the throne early in the 12th century, recovered Pomerania, which had been lost by his predecessors. But the next generation of rulers, Bolesaw the Wry's five sons, divided Poland between them, with the largest share going to the oldest, Ladislav II. Internal squabbling fissured the country further, as rival dukes sought to expand their holdings. Although successive monarchs occupied a throne in Poland's capital, Kraków, they governed in name only. No longer a united country, Poland was a prime target for invasion. In 1241 Tatars—warriors from Russia—moved in, leaving large areas of Poland in ruins. Then the country's northern duchies buckled under the onslaught of Lithuanians and Prussians—neighboring peoples who had not yet adopted Christianity.

From Division to Unity

In the 13th century, Poland suffered repeated invasions, and in 1226 Prince Conrad, who reigned over the principality of Mazovia, situated east of the Vistula River, sought the assistance of the Teutonic Knights. A band of Germanic soldiers who had fought in the Crusades, these knights soon proved to be plunderers and marauders. They responded to Conrad's request by ousting the Prussians, but then seized the land for themselves, carving their own state out of the con-

Conrad von Thuringen, grand master of the Teutonic Knights, is portrayed in a 13th-century tomb relief.

During the 14th century Poland's King Casimir III was widely known as a benevolent monarch.

quered provinces. The knights imported settlers from Germany, who erected and inhabited towns that answered to German laws and followed German customs. By 1308 this Teutonic domain cut off the rest of Poland from its northern outlet, the Baltic Sea.

Meanwhile, the native peasants of Poland sank into serfdom—enslavement to the land and to the nobles who reaped the larger part of their harvests. Like many people in the Middle Ages, the serfs found solace in the church. Its promise of hope in the afterlife eased the drudgery of farm work, and its all encompassing worldview imposed order on the vagaries of daily existence.

Just as Poland's peasants suffered, so did the nation itself, parceled among outsiders who wrung the land for all it was worth. Gradually, the resentments of the native population cohered into organized resistance and then a unification movement. Wladyslaw the Short, who came from north-central Poland, succeeded in unifying much of the country, and in 1320 was crowned Wladyslaw I. The nation made even greater strides under his son, Casimir III (1333–70). The last in the long line of Piast's direct successors, Casimir III was also the only Polish king to be designated "the Great." It has been said that Casimir III found a Poland built of wood and left a nation built of stone.

Casimir's achievements were many. He acquired territory to the east, bettered the lot of peasants, opened

After 1569, Lithuanian peasants shared the political fortunes of their counterparts in Poland.

During the 16th century Nicolaus Copernicus pioneered the science of modern astronomy.

the country to Jews (who had suffered persecution throughout western Europe), and in the Statutes of Wislica codified the nation's laws in a way that summarized all the legal customs and practices of the past and provided the basis for all future legislation. In addition, Casimir ordered the construction of stone castles, which shored up the country's defenses, and also erected educational institutions (including the first Polish university, built in Kraków in 1347), churches, city halls, and cathedrals of fresh white stone carved into lofty Gothic spires and arches. He authorized the introduction of silver currency, which encouraged commercial trade, and provided protection for the peasants and for the Jews, two groups that had been badly treated throughout much of Polish history.

After Casimir's death, the scepter was passed on to his nephew, Louis I of Hungary. He granted increased privileges to the nobility, who in turn promised that one of his daughters would succeed him as monarch. The promise was kept and after Louis's death, his daughter Jadwiga took the throne. She wed Jagiello, grand duke of neighboring Lithuania, a land bordering the Baltic Sea. More than a personal union, the marriage merged the two nations for nearly 200 years. United with Poland, Lithuania evolved from its previous pagan state. In due course, all but the lowest levels of society became Polonized—in language and in outlook. The combined forces of Poland and Lithuania ousted the Teutonic Order, and Poland regained access to the Baltic Sea.

King Sigismund II Augustus helped stem the tide of Protestantism in northern Europe by encouraging reform within Poland's Catholic church.

Three Wise Men

In the 16th century, Poland entered its golden age. One of the largest nations in Europe, it enjoyed power and prestige. It had progressed far enough to contribute handsomely to the Renaissance, the revival of learning that flourished across the Continent. Kraków became a center of art, culture, and scholarship, primarily through the achievements of three great men. Nicolaus Copernicus (1473–1543) overturned prevailing concepts of the earth's place in the universe by proving that the earth revolved around the sun. Poet Jan Kochanowski (1530–84) is generally credited with founding a literary tradition in the Polish language. Jan Zamojski (1542–1605), a student of ancient Roman history, became the architect of Poland's "noble democracy." These three wise men represented the best and the brightest, and belonged to what was probably the most inspiring era in Polish history.

The Respublica

In 1569 the Treaty of Lublin formalized the marriage of Poland and Lithuania. The two countries agreed to maintain their separate laws and administrations and agreed also to be governed jointly by an elected king and by the *Sejm*, a ruling body that had a senate (representing powerful landowners and clergy) and a chamber (representing the lesser nobility and landowners).

The nobility accumulated even more power in 1572 with the death of King Sigismund II, the last Jagiello ruler. Thereafter, kings could gain the throne only if elected and no Polish dynasty emerged in the following centuries. The new government, called the *Respublica*—the United Republic of Poland-Lithuania—lasted about 200 years, ruled by 11 elected kings, each of whom reigned for an average of 20 years. During this time, the nation lost its strength. Kings, because they answered to the nobility, surrendered most of their authority. Unless the Sejm consented, no monarch could wage war, raise taxes, or choose his own spouse. If he

violated these laws even once, the nation disowned him.

To the modern mind, this seems an equitable system. Instead of cowering before an imperial autocrat, individual Poles—or at least privileged nobles—shaped the nation's policy. In reality, the system weakened Poland drastically, leaving it ill equipped to fend off other nations, most of which were centralized monarchies eager to widen their borders in almost any direction. At one time or another, Poland found itself at war with Russia, Sweden, and Turkey, conflicts that eroded its territory, depleted its coffers, and reduced its manpower.

These losses compounded Poland's internal woes. A telling blow came in 1652, with the advent of the *liberum veto*, a parliamentary innovation that enabled a

The Sejm, Poland's parliament, granted exceptional power to individual noblemen.

single dissenting legislator to block passage of any bill and also to dissolve the Sejm, postponing all decisions until the next session. In effect, this entrusted to each legislator the fate of the nation's policy and made Poland susceptible to meddlesome foreign powers, who often bribed noblemen to act against the country's best interests. The prized liberties of the noblemen thus festered into untrammeled license.

Inevitably, the republic slid toward decadence and the nobility fell into sloth. The 19th-century English writer Thomas Carlyle described Poland's republic as a "beautifully phosphorescent rot-heap," fed upon by a parasitic nobility. This group—called the *Szlachta*—obeyed a strict code of chivalry scorned in many other parts of Europe. The Szlachta idealized their aristocratic "blue blood" and practiced what one historian has called "noble racism." Joined by their elitism, all noblemen addressed one another as "brother," and all

A political cartoon from 1774 satirizes the first partition of Poland, the "plumcake," by greedy European monarchs.

were entitled to the same privileges regardless of wealth.

The middle class in Poland was composed of merchants, many of them Germans and Jews. Indeed Poland, which later became notorious for its anti-Semitism, showed relative tolerance toward this group for many centuries. A small population of Jews lived there as early as the 10th century, and during the period of the republic the numbers steadily climbed. Still, the Jews did not feel overly comfortable or secure. Polish law isolated Jews from the rest of the population by barring them from owning land. This restriction meant that Jews could not earn a living as landlords or farmers. Thus they became merchants and professionals—doctors, lawyers, accountants, and moneylenders—and as such figured importantly in the nation's economy. At the same time Jews remained culturally apart: They had their own religion and often sent their children to Jewish schools. Many spoke only Yiddish, and no Polish, which angered nationalistic Poles.

By the 17th century anti-Semitism became more widespread, culminating in two *pogroms*—racist massacres—the first in 1648, the second in 1769. Despite these violent outbursts, Poland generally remained multicultural and multiethnic.

The Republic Crumbles

Some of Poland's groups coexisted uneasily, however. Almost as soon as Poland and Lithuania united, discord developed between Poland's Roman Catholics and Lithuanians who belonged to the Greek (or Eastern) Orthodox church and felt an allegiance to Russia. In 1667 Russia, Prussia, and Austria, the most powerful nations in eastern Europe, decided to unite and conquer the Polish republic. Even as they subjugated the Poles, the leaders of the three nations—Catherine, empress of Russia; Frederick, king of Prussia; and Joseph II, emperor of Austria—fought among themselves. The strongest of the three, Catherine, planned for the Polish republic to remain a weak and impoverished child, dependent on nearby "mother Russia." To accomplish this she blocked any attempt at political improvement in Poland, and by doing so drove the frustrated reformers into rebellion. These actions unsettled the Austrians and the Prussians and forced Catherine into territorial concessions.

The year 1772 proved fateful. It was then that the first partition of Poland took place. Russia took Lithuania; Prussia, Pomerania; Austria, Galicia. The second partition occurred a year later, in 1793, when Poland lost Podolia and Volhynia and what little remained of its holdings in Lithuania. A courageous general named Dabrowski organized the Poles who had emigrated to other European countries into a Polish Legion, a government in exile, and in 1795 patriot Thaddeus Kosciuszko led a revolt, but both efforts were unsuccessful. The greed and jealousy of Poland's imperialist neighbors culminated in the third partition of 1795, which completely carved up the old Poland and wiped the country from the map. In 1815, at the Congress of Vienna, the area was repartitioned, with Kraków established as the Kingdom of Poland.

A Nation in Pieces

In 1905 Polish nationalist Marshal Josef Pilsudski led an insurrection in Warsaw, which was put down by the Russians. He fled to Kraków and in 1908 organized legions of Polish youth who fought beside Austro-Hungarian troops against the Russians in 1914. But the very

next year Austrians and Germans defeated the Polish legions and Poland was split into a German and an Austrian zone, only to be reunified again in 1916. In 1917 the Poles in exile battled the new government. Poland was reestablished as a nation, with Marshal Pilsudski installed as head of state, and Ignacy Jan Paderewski, a renowned concert pianist, named premier (he had been head of the Polish government in exile). The Polish map now included the same lands as in 1772—before the partitions. After World War I ended in 1918,

Initially a socialist, Marshal Jozef Pilsudski ended his career as a right-wing dictator, backed by the Polish military.

the Versailles treaty awarded Poland most of West Prussia and what became known as the Polish Corridor—a strip of land that had previously belonged to Germany and gave Poland much-needed access to the Baltic Sea. Poland was also forced to sign the 1919 Minority Treaty, a pact that guaranteed the rights of all minorities in the defeated countries. But the Poles refused to obey the antidiscriminatory rules of the treaty and continued to treat the Jews as separate and unequal. In 1922 Pilsudski stepped down, but four years later he resumed his rule and became virtual dictator until his death in 1935. Marshal Edward Rydz-Smigly, a Pilsudski supporter, continued the dictatorship.

The Holocaust

On September 1, 1939, World War II began when German troops marched into Poland. Two weeks later, Germany's temporary ally, the Soviet Union, led by Joseph Stalin, invaded Poland from the east, advancing

Ignacy Jan Paderewski addresses a crowd in 1918.

In 1919, Jewish-American veterans of World War I protested the persecution of Polish Jews.

to Kraków. In 1941 Hitler violated his pact with Stalin, attacking Russia, and Poland fell entirely under German dominion. The German leader, Nazi dictator Adolph Hitler, had not even bothered to declare war on a nation his armies nearly annihilated. Some 6 million Poles died during Germany's invasion and occupation, and 2.5 million more were shipped to forced-labor camps in Germany.

The most severe damage was wrought on Poland's Jews. Poland had the highest concentration of Jews in all of Europe—40 percent of the continent's total Jewish population in the 1930s. For this reason the Nazis made Poland the main target of their anti-Semitic campaign. When the Nazis entered Poland they confined anyone who had three Jewish grandparents—even Jews who had converted to Catholicism—in ghettos, sections of cities that German troops cordoned off and guarded closely. Death awaited any Jew discovered outside the ghetto, and the same fate greeted any Pole caught helping a Jew escape. By war's end, only about 100,000 Polish Jews had survived, out of a total population that had exceeded 3.1 million.

German troops invade Poland in 1939.

In the darkest chapter of Polish history, some Poles collaborated with the Nazis, helping identify Jews who had eluded the Nazis' detection. This devastating betrayal had its origins in centuries of animosity between Poland's Jews and its larger Christian population.

The Nazis themselves eventually removed Jews from the ghettos—especially in Bodz, Warsaw, and Bialystok, which had the largest Jewish populations—and placed them in concentration camps all over Poland. There they imposed the "final solution" to the "Jewish question." This euphemism disguised a policy of extermination: Jews in concentration camps were herded by the hundreds into showers that sprayed not water, but poisonous gas. By the end of the war the Nazis had murdered more than 6 million Jews throughout Europe.

Some brave Poles assisted the Jews. Known as Righteous Christians, these Poles risked their lives helping Jews elude the Nazis. After the war ended, the newly founded state of Israel created a memorial to them, *Yad va shem*, a walk lined with trees, each planted to commemorate a Christian who risked his or her life to help save a Jew. Righteous Christians came from all classes and backgrounds. Some were peasants, some intellectuals. The most celebrated of all Righteous Christians was Raoul Wallenberg, a Swedish aristocrat personally responsible for saving hundreds of Jewish lives.

One Jew who survived because of the efforts of her Polish compatriots was Nechama Tec. She was a young Jewish girl in Poland when the Nazis invaded. Because Nechama and her sister both had blond hair and blue eyes, they managed to pass for Christians. They lived with a Polish family and eventually fled to the United States. Nechama Tec became a professor of sociology at Fairfield University in Connecticut. Her book *Dry Tears* describes what it was like to be a Jewish girl passing for a Christian, to live in a time and place when a trip to the corner store to buy bread could turn into a death sentence.

From August 1 to October 2, 1944, Jews confined to the Warsaw ghetto staged a battle against the Nazis, who later forced the leaders of the uprising into concentration camps.

In 1983, Polish opposition leader Lech Walesa is cheered by fellow workers as he leaves the Gdańsk shipyards.

A Soviet Satellite

As Germany devastated Poland, some Poles fought to make their country independent. Exiles formed a resistance movement centered in France, then England. It included some prisoners of war released by the Soviet Union who then joined the Allied forces. In 1944 Russian troops entered Poland and allowed a provisional Polish government to govern in Lublin. Another Polish resistance movement arose in Warsaw, but the Nazis destroyed it. In 1945 the last Nazis were chased from the country, and Russia took control of it. Later that year the Yalta Conference ratified the Soviet claim to Poland and redefined the Russian-Polish border. The Potsdam Conference of 1945 placed more territory—including Gdańsk—back in Polish hands. In 1946 a parliament was established by general vote, and the next year Boleslaw Beruit, a Pole who belonged to the Communist party, became the nation's president.

Thereafter Poland reluctantly became a Soviet satellite. Relations between the two countries often grew strained. In 1956 students and workers rioted in Poznań, denouncing Stalin's dictatorial policies. The protest paid off—Poles gained more freedom, and the government expelled some especially zealous Communists. Poland retained its alliance with the Soviet Union, however. In 1970 more riots occurred, this time in cities on the Baltic Sea, where workers protested soaring food costs.

A decade later, the most remarkable show of independence occurred when dockworkers in Gdańsk began a strike that spread to other industries throughout the nation. The walkouts proved so successful that the Polish government gave in to the strikers' demands for an independent union—the first ever allowed in a communist country. A year later another strike occurred, spearheaded by Solidarity, a Gdańsk labor union that pressed for increased personal freedoms and an improved standard of living.

This strike toppled the existing government and led to the emergence of a new premier, General Wojciech Jaruzelski, who declared martial law, outlawed strikes, and imprisoned Solidarity leaders, including the organization's founder, Lech Walesa, a dockworker who became an international hero. Named Man of the Year by *Time* magazine in 1982 and awarded the Nobel Peace Prize in 1983, Walesa symbolized the power of the ordinary citizen to redress the wrongs of a tyrannical government.

But even Walesa and his vast celebrity could not slow the gears of the Soviet machine. In 1984 a pro-Solidarity priest, Jerzy Popeilusko, was abducted and murdered by secret police. And in 1987 repression continued against heads of labor unions, intellectuals, writers, journalists, and people in the fine arts. Today's Poles have many reasons for leaving their homeland—so did their forebears, as the next chapter shows. ✎

Two Polish peasants view their livestock on a farm near the Russian border in 1924.

REASONS TO LEAVE

Poles may have been among the first Europeans ever to journey to the New World. Some evidence suggests that Poles possibly sailed with the Viking ships thought to have reached North America in the 11th century, and scholars have theorized that a few Poles made the transatlantic journey with Christopher Columbus in 1492. The German ship *Mary and Margaret*, which in 1608 arrived at the English settlement in Jamestown, Virginia, included Poles who helped develop the timber industry in the colonies.

The Spirit of '76

Poles began to arrive in force during the American Revolution. The colonists' fight for their independence did indeed produce "a shot heard around the world." The glorious cause attracted Polish adventurers, radicals, and revolutionaries, and believers in the right of a people to govern themselves. Few of these Poles intended to settle permanently in North America. Among those who arrived during this period, two became heroes still revered by Polish Americans, and throughout the United States their names grace monuments and bridges and appear on the mastheads of fraternal organizations and businesses.

Count Casimir Pulaski, born in 1747, belonged to a noble family in Poland. In 1768 he and his father formed a confederation that sought to free Poland of Russian influence by rebelling against King Stanislaw II, a pawn of Moscow. Russian troops quashed the confederation's troops in 1772, and the younger Pulaski fled to Turkey, Prussia, and eventually France, where in 1775 he met Benjamin Franklin, who was in Paris on a diplomatic mission to drum up support for the American Revolution. Franklin gave Pulaski a letter of introduction to George Washington, and the Pole set off across the Atlantic in 1777. Joining the colonial forces, he organized his own cavalry command and fought valiantly until the British attack on Savannah, where he was mortally wounded in 1779.

Another Polish-American hero, Thaddeus Kosciuszko, was born in 1746. After attending military schools in Warsaw and Paris, Kosciuszko offered his services to the American revolutionaries. He fought with distinction, then returned to Poland to help the cause of independence in 1792–93. A year later, he assembled forces that led a national rebellion against Russia and Prussia. The effort failed and Kosciuszko, after a brief term of imprisonment, went back to the United States, serving as liaison between Thomas Jefferson and the leaders of France, which staged its own revolution in 1789. A champion of black rights, Kosciuszko authorized Jefferson in his last will and testament—dated May 5, 1789—to sell off his property and with the monies earned provide for slaves:

I, Thaddeus Kosciuszko, being just on my departure from America, do hereby declare and direct that, should I make no other testamentary disposition of my property in the United States, I hereby authorize my friend Thomas Jefferson to employ the whole thereof in purchasing Negroes from among his own or any other and giving them liberty in my name; in giving them education in trade or otherwise; in having them instructed for their new condition in the duties of morality which may make them good neighbors, good

Thaddeus Kosciuszko attained the rank of general in the Polish army.

fathers and mothers, husbands and wives, in their duty as citizens; teaching them to be defenders of their liberty and country, of the good order of society, and in whatsoever may make them happy and useful.

Kosciuszko died in 1817. His bequest helped found a "Colored School" at Newark, New Jersey, in 1826, named after its benefactor.

The Next Wave

The Poles who joined Kosciuszko in the attempt to win Poland's independence studied the events unfolding in

An engraving by F. Girsch shows George Washington with the foreign officers who fought in the revolutionary war.

America, alert for clues that might help them change the situation in their homeland, which had been partitioned by Prussia, Russia, and Germany. In 1830, Poles rose up against the dictatorial and paternalistic rule of Russian czar Nicholas I. The uprising—known as the November Revolution—resulted in much bloodshed. Russian troops marched into Warsaw, and the government in Moscow suspended the Polish constitution. About 1,000 Poles escaped to the United States on British ships that sailed from Prussia. After another uprising in 1863, when the Russians instituted a Russification policy to make the Polish people adopt Russian culture, Poles fled to European capitals such as Geneva, Paris, and London, and American metropolises such as New York, Chicago, and San Francisco.

During the period of unrest in Poland, a number of Americans, among them the writer Edgar Allan Poe, offered to serve the Polish cause, looking for what he called "an appointment in the Polish Army . . . in the event of the interference of France in behalf of Poland." The Polish American Committee in Paris raised a large sum for the Polish rebels, soliciting the funds through an appeal drafted by the American novelist James Fenimore Cooper. Cooper's passionate interest in helping Poland began in 1830, when he met the Polish poet Adam Mickiewicz in Rome. Mickiewicz also greatly impressed the American inventor Samuel F.B. Morse, and he too joined the cause. After the November 1830 uprising, political exiles conceived the idea of setting up a new Poland in America. They summoned their compatriots with these words:

> Poles! Let us leave that wretched country now no more our own though soaked with the blood of her best defenders . . . . America is the only country worthy of affording an asylum to men who have sacrificed everything for freedom. There Poland will be enshrined in our hearts, and Heaven will perhaps bless our devotion.

Sir Casimir S. Growski, an insurrectionist in the Polish uprising of 1830, later immigrated to North America, where he helped develop the Canadian railroad and also assisted in building the International Bridge, which spans the Niagara River.

Crossing the Atlantic

Groups of Polish expatriates started arriving in America in 1834, but the communities they established did not always succeed. For example, on December 21, 1849, the sailing ship *Manchester* departed from Le Havre, France, for a long and wearisome voyage to New Orleans, Louisiana. The ship's passengers included the first community of Polish immigrants—105 men, women, and children—living in France as a consequence of the November uprising. The immigrants' leader, a 54-year-old doctor named Francis Lawrynowicz, planned to set up a colony of adjacent farms in Louisiana. But shortly after the group arrived there, yellow fever blanketed the state, killing thousands, among them the settlers led by Dr. Lawrynowicz.

Despite failure such as this, the United States encouraged further immigration, especially after the American Civil War depleted the nation's economic and cultural resources. In his Fourth Annual Message in 1864, President Abraham Lincoln said, "I regard our immigrants as one of the principal replenishing streams which are appointed by providence to repair the ravages of internal war and its waste of national strength and health."

Throughout Polish history, land had always been the key to security. Owning property meant stability, losing it meant ruin. The Poles believed that "a man without land is like a man without legs; he crawls about and cannot get anywhere." Peasant families tended to be large, providing many hands to work in the fields. In the second half of the 19th century, Poland's agricultural economy weakened as the United States and the western European countries developed advanced methods of planting and harvesting that enabled them to produce food more cheaply. Too poor to implement these new techniques, Polish peasant farmers lagged behind in the international marketplace. As profits plummeted, the Poles lost their land, and many went

Michael Goldwasser, a Polish merchant of Jewish ancestry, immigrated to California after the insurrection of 1848.

hungry. The large families that once had made farming efficient suddenly meant a surplus of mouths to feed.

These conditions caused the greatest Polish immigration to the United States. Sometimes called *za chlebem*—or "for-bread" immigrants—these people did not plan to settle permanently in America. They hoped they could save enough money to return to Poland and build a better life. In the words of one young immigrant, a 26-year-old Polish Catholic:

> I intend to go in a few days to a Jewish agent in Konstantynow to make an arrangement for crossing the frontier without a passport, for I am absolutely deter-

mined to go now to New York or Philadelphia to earn some hundreds of roubles there within 2 or 3 years then to come back to our country and rent a mill or buy a piece of land with the money collected in this way.

Other Poles, however, had given up on their homeland. To them living conditions seemed unbearable, and the possibilities for change hopeless. One disillusioned Pole, 24 years old and married, wrote:

I have a very great wish to go to America. I want to leave my native country because we are 6 children and we have very little land, only about 6 morgs [about 13 acres] and some small farm-buildings, so that our whole farm is worth 1200 roubles at the highest. And my parents are still young; father is 48 and mother 42 years old. So it is difficult for us to live . . . Here in our country one must work plenty and wages are very small, just enough to live, so I would like to go in the name of our Lord God; perhaps I would earn more there.

An Austrian print from the 1870s satirizes Jewish emigration agents swindling Polish peasants.

Another immigrant echoed these sentiments:

I want to go to America, but I have no means at all beause I am poor and having nothing but the ten

fingers of my hands, a wife and 9 children. I have no work at all, although I am strong and healthy and only 45 years old. I cannot earn for my family. I have been already in Dabrowa, Sosnowiec, Zawiercie and Lodz, wherever I could go, and nowhere could I earn well. And here the children call for food and clothing and more or less education. I wish to work, not easily only but even hard, but what can I do? I will not go to steal and I have no work.

The brave Poles who gambled everything they had in the hope of making a fresh start in North America did not act entirely on their own. Support often came from a vast and efficient letter-writing network that linked the Old World and the New. This network also helped preserve a record of the immigrants' experiences, giving posterity insight into lives such as the one led by Kathryn Wyrzkowski, a Pole from the Prussian region of Poland who came to the United States at the age of 18.

After a 48-day voyage that began in France, Kathryn Wyrzkowski passed through the immigration center at New York City's Castle Garden on July 16, 1850. She headed to Shamokin, Pennsylvania, a small area nestled in the heart of mining country. She found a job as a servant in a boardinghouse, then sent letters to her father, brothers, sisters, other relatives, and friends, urging them to join her. Before long they came, and within four years a community of Polish settlers grew in Shamokin and surrounding areas. This pattern of one person coming over and writing home about the New World became common in areas all over the United States.

The letters newcomers mailed to the Old World varied greatly, from missives of hope to tearstained laments of loneliness and alienation. Their readers back in Poland, struggling to survive, took heart when they learned of abundant opportunities in America. Even if life there involved hardship, it offered something different from what they knew, and descriptions of it did more to bring Poles to America than anything else.

At Ellis Island, Polish immigrants in quarantine dance beneath a multilingual sign, informing them that their meals will be free of charge.

Other inducements to travel to the New World sprang from less pure motives. Greedy railroad and steamship companies distributed brochures featuring exaggerated accounts of the possibilities to be found across the Atlantic. In addition, hundreds of agents commissioned by the companies scoured Poland's cities and rural areas for potential immigrants. Soon this form of enticement became a lucrative business, not only in Poland but throughout Europe. Many peasants and farmers sold all their possessions—land, livestock, and personal effects—to finance passage to America. Most arrived with only spare change and the names of friends who might have already moved halfway across the huge country.

Most of the Poles who came over at this time traveled in steerage—the crowded holds of American-bound cargo ships. The experience on board often proved more alarming than any hardship awaiting them in the United States. Crammed into filthy quarters, the immigrants fell prey to seasickness, infectious disease, and frequent outbursts of violence. The steamship companies soon realized that in order to maintain a steady flow of passengers they had to be more selective about issuing tickets. They turned away convicts, prostitutes, lunatics, and cripples, as well as immigrants afflicted with goiter, trachoma, syphilis, and other contagious diseases. If infirm passengers somehow filtered through the screening procedures and survived the arduous voyage, they faced further challenges when they finally landed.

The Lady of the Harbor

Poles came over in waves, gathering momentum as the 20th century dawned. In 1899 Poles ranked fourth among the population of new arrivals. In 1900 they surpassed the Irish and took third place. At this time,

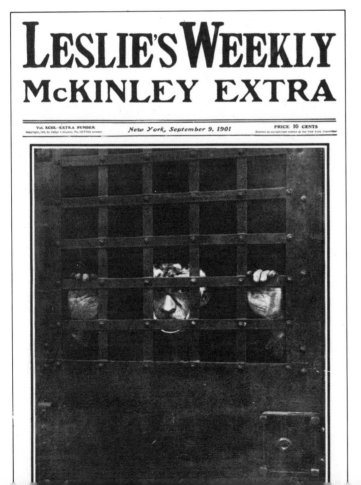

LESLIE'S WEEKLY
McKINLEY EXTRA

Vol. XCIII.—EXTRA NUMBER.
Copyright, 1901, by Judge Company, No. 110 Fifth Avenue

New York, September 9, 1901

PRICE 10 CENTS
Entered as second-class matter at the New York Post-Office

President McKinley's assassin, Leon F. Czolgosz, an anarchist of Polish descent, peers out from behind prison bars in 1901.

10 percent of all immigrants were Polish. Between 1870 and 1914, more than 2 million Poles immigrated to the United States.

They joined a massive European tide. From 1855 to 1890, 8 million newcomers landed at Castle Garden, a refurbished military post where new arrivals submitted to a battery of examinations. Doctors probed their bodies and appraised their mental health, and customs officials judged a more nebulous quality—the immigrants' ability to support themselves in the New World. Though these various stages of inspection seemed impartial and efficient, they amounted in fact to a maze of corruption that wide-eyed newcomers negotiated with extreme trouble and pain. Brutality, graft, and bribery became so routine at the state-operated facility that one official described the entire process as "a perfect farce." Finally the federal government stepped in, taking power away from the state, and Congress enacted a law that prevented indiscriminate rejection of immigrants.

Hopeful immigrants apply for entry permits at the United States embassy in Warsaw sometime during the 1920s.

In 1892 the government built a new facility on Ellis Island to process the throngs of foreigners who disembarked in New York Bay. There, immigrants—Poles,

Irish, Italians, Norwegians, Germans, and many others—all awaited admittance to the promised land. Some of these hopefuls came in good health; others were ailing; some spoke English, others did not. The hustle and bustle was fueled by fear: Would they be let in? A 1913 arrival from Russia, Stephen Grahm, wrote, "The day of the emigrants' arrival in New York was the nearest earthly likeness to the final day of judgment, when we have to prove our fitness to enter."

Many failed in the effort. Today we can only guess at the pain felt by families wrenched apart at the discretion of immigration authorities. Children and mothers were torn from each other's arms, as were husbands and wives, sisters and brothers. Officially, Ellis Island served as the immigrants' point of entry into the United States. In reality, "the island of tears" gave the immigrants a taste of what the nation itself held in store for them. In some ways, the immigration center represented a melting pot—the symbol of America's tolerance for peoples of different origins, but at the same time it operated with bureaucratic indifference. Similarly, the Statue of Liberty—"the Lady of the Harbor"—beckoned to the tired and poor of Europe, but not if they bore marks of disease and not if they lacked the means to support themselves and their families in the New World.

Under the best of circumstances, Polish immigrants would have been unsettled by the New World, but a political incident made matters even more difficult. In 1901 President William A. McKinley was assassinated by Leon F. Czolgosz, a young man of Polish parentage and radical political leanings. This incident caused a backlash of anti-Polish sentiment and triggered a chain of events, most pointedly a bill introduced in Congress to keep out anarchists (especially those from eastern Europe). According to historian Frank Mocha, "The two shots [Czolgosz] fired on a sunny September afternoon in 1901 produced results more far reaching than many wars." ❧

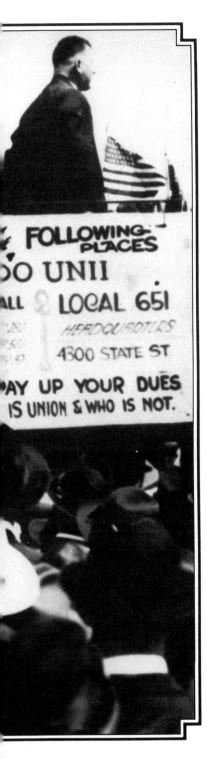

Polish workers gather in Chicago during the mid-20th century.

LIFE IN AMERICA

Polish immigrants had many obstacles to hurdle. Acting individually, the new arrivals might have felt overwhelmed, but by forming communities they managed to help one another out. As one immigrant wrote to his family back home: "I have work, I'm not hungry, only I have not yet laughed since I came to America . . . . But come and see that here no one goes to bed on an empty stomach because one Pole will save another, if he can."

In 1854 Father Leopold Moczygemba, a Franciscan monk, led a group of 800 men, women, and children to a Texas town they named Panna Maria (Polish for the Virgin Mary). The colonists established a church and a school, where the organist taught the three Rs (in Polish), the pastor taught religion, and a native-born American instructed the children in the English language and in sewing. Panna Maria grew and prospered, the first of a number of Polish settlements in Texas.

Across the country, Polish immigrants founded farming colonies, many capitalizing on the American government's attempts to lure pioneers west. The 1862 Homestead Act made 160 acres available free of charge to anyone—born in America or overseas—willing to clear and live on the land in the country's western territories.

Yet the vast majority of Polish immigrants wanted to leave farming behind and find a new livelihood. Pennsylvania mining towns, such as Wilkes-Barre and

Father Leopold Moczygemba poses for a photograph, c. 1860.

Hazleton, employed unskilled laborers, as did the steel centers of Pittsburgh and Cleveland. Polish immigrants also gravitated to the mills, slaughterhouses, refineries, and foundries of Toledo, Ohio; South Bend, Indiana; Milwaukee, Wisconsin; Minneapolis-St. Paul, Minnesota; Omaha, Nebraska; St. Louis, Missouri; and Chicago, Illinois. Large Polish communities also sprang up in New York, Buffalo, and Detroit.

For men who had worked outdoors their whole lives, laboring in underground mines or sweltering foundries required difficult adjustments. As historian Herbert Gurman has pointed out, farm labor obeyed certain natural rhythms: The workday paralleled the daylight hours, and changing weather prohibited constant toil, as did the seasons. But in America, factory life knew no natural time frame. The workday bore no relation to natural daylight and thus threatened the laborers' health. Polish men accepted these conditions, eschewing lighter jobs, such as needlework, which they contemptuously referred to as "women's work." Most tended to seek industrial employment, which involved various dangers. Many operated heavy machinery that cost them life and limb. A New York Department of Labor survey from 1902–03 listed the following casualties:

Pobish, Michael; helper in print shop, 26 years of age; married; . . . instantly killed on December 21, 1902, while painting runway of electric traveling crane in erecting shop; crane crushing body so badly so as to expose heart to view . . . Walazinovice, Simon; floor helper; 38 years of age; married; . . . fatally injured on April 7, 1903, in the tank shop; while helping unload

Slaughterhouse workers stir a vat of boiling pigs.

boiler plate, clamp slipped off plate which was suspended in air by lifting crane, and fell on Walazinovice, badly crushing abdomen and lower portion of body; death resulted almost immediately . . .

Both these men were married, as were the majority of adult men, and Walazinovice left five children and an aggrieved widow behind. When such disasters struck, Polish Americans needed most to pull together as a community.

Getting Respect

After struggling to find a place to settle and a means of support, Polish immigrants faced yet another obstacle: Their American neighbors did not always welcome them with open arms. The record numbers of newcomers frightened many native-born Americans and also earlier immigrant generations who feared for their jobs and the stability of their neighborhoods. American newspapers complained loudly of "the mixed populations with which we are afflicted." Anyone who spoke halting or broken English became fair game for ridicule and discrimination. Employers sometimes withheld wages or paid the newcomers less than they deserved.

Sausage makers practice their craft at a meat-packing house.

Shopkeepers overcharged them for food, clothing, and other necessities. Landlords sometimes provided lodging that was neither clean nor comfortable. John J. Bukowczyk's *And My Children Do Not Know Me*, a history of Polish Americans, quotes an anonymous letter sent to the homeland from Brooklyn, New York, bemoaning the conditions that greeted Poles in the New World:

> What people from America write to Poland is all bluster; there is not a word of truth. For in America Poles work like cattle. Where a dog does not want to sit, there the Pole is made to sit, and the poor wretch works because he wants to eat.

A 1920 photograph shows the wife of a Slavic miner in Pennsylvania doing the weekly wash.

Nonetheless, many immigrants decided to chance the rough journey across the Atlantic, despite having been forewarned by letters detailing the hardships and prejudice in the New World.

First Steps

Most of the first immigrants were young men, who came singly or in groups. Such an immigrant usually carried only a small amount of money—in the late 19th century the average Polish newcomer brought less than $14. Some of the luckier travelers also had a piece of paper with the address of a relative or friend written on it. Sometimes, however, the location was transcribed so poorly from English to Polish that native-born Americans were at a loss to guide immigrants to their desired destination. One Polish boy arrived at Ellis Island with an address that read:

Pittsburgh, Pa., Panewna
Stait 16 Babereia 47

After two hours of deciphering, a kind and patient secretary at Pittsburgh's Young Men's Christian Association (YMCA) produced the correct address:

Penn Ave., 16th Street
47 Mulberry Alley

Often young immigrants took public transportation—wrestling with schedules and complicated directions—to a boardinghouse that had been recommended by friends or relatives. The system of boardinghouses—called *trzymanie bortnikow*—became an important feature of Polish-American life in the early 1900s. Bed and meals cost from two to three dollars per month, and the boarders often interacted like a family. The houses themselves resembled Old World residences, with backyards roamed by pigs, goats, chickens, and cows, much to the dismay of neighbors. Boardinghouses were usually located near the places where the men found work—in coal or steel mines or in factories in the poorer sections of towns and cities. In *Natives and Strangers*, a survey of America's ethnic groups, historians Leonard Dinnerstein, Roger L. Nichols, and David M. Reimers describe the Polish district in Chicago as "nothing more than an infested wall-to-wall carpet of rotted wood and crumbling concrete."

Many towns in the Midwest and parts of the Northeast developed Polish-American communities that became self-supporting. As their populations grew, an increasing number of Poles congregated in central areas, bringing a wide variety of useful skills. Shoemakers and dressmakers, butchers and bakers set up shops that served the ethnic community and also bound its members together. This fellowship led in turn to mutual aid societies that immigrants could appeal to in the event of emergencies and that, in effect, amounted to a transported and modernized version of the homeland the Poles had left behind.

This cohesiveness also characterized Polish-American families, which depended on every member accepting a fair share of the load. The workday began at sunrise and lasted late into the night—even for children, who took jobs at the earliest possible age and learned from birth to put their family's survival ahead of their own ambitions. The pressure to keep the family fed and clothed left little time for any activity other than work. A hefty portion of each family's income went toward supporting an institution that figured importantly in the life of the Polish-American community: the church.

Priest-Titans

The local parish invariably served as the focal point of the community. It catered to religious needs—transported for the most part intact from Poland—and also provided a social center, a network for fledgling fraternal organizations. When immigrants faced poverty or eviction or simply needed comfort they often turned to the men who presided over their parishes—the priests. So powerful and influential did these clerics become that some people cynically referred to them as "priest-titans." Most immigrants willingly accorded their priests this exalted status, but some drew pointed comparisons between the church in Polonia and the rigid institution that dominated Poland in the Middle Ages.

Indeed, the religion had not changed much since then and Poles continued to differ from some other Roman Catholics in a number of ways, though they shared with their Italian coreligionists a devout veneration of the Virgin Mary (whom the Poles referred to

as "Poland's Queen"). The Poles venerated their own saints, spoke Polish during religious ceremonies, and celebrated certain rites in a traditional way that kept alive a heritage that traced back nearly 1,000 years. In North America, they built their own churches and often tried to persuade priests and nuns in the homeland t leave their secure stations and fill posts in the New World. One reason America's Polish Catholics wanted to beef up their clergy was that the community resented the domination of Irish-American Catholics. Over time however, the Polish-Catholic church gained strength.

Milwaukee's "Little Poland" was one of many Polish neighborhoods that sprang up across the Midwest during th 1800s.

Immigrants from eastern Europe were often forced to live in squalid tenement buildings.

As one Polish American characterized the situation, "Without the Church we have lost our identity."

The Women

Although the immigrants retained much of their Old World values, they did not want Polonia to be a mirror of Poland, a country that, after all, they had fled. Women, especially, responded to the freedom offered by America. Frequently left behind by husbands who crossed the ocean to scout out North America or, after arriving, pressed on to new parts of the country to explore job opportunities, women gained something they had never had before: control over the family.

Forced to support themselves and their children, many became breadwinners. They ran their own businesses, usually boardinghouses or laundries, which enabled them to earn money without leaving home. Young girls without family responsibilities found jobs in factories or as domestic servants. Some women performed numerous tasks at once. *Natives and Strangers* includes an account of a West Virginia Polish immigrant who operated a boardinghouse for miners while carrying a child. One night she awoke at 3:00 A.M. to give birth, then rose 3 hours later to prepare breakfast and box lunches for 13 boarders. For Polish-American women, childbearing was perhaps the most trying burden. Because their Catholic faith forbade them to practice birth control, the typical Polish-American mother bore 5 to 10 children under primitive conditions that endangered mother and child alike.

Education

Work placed such a strain on every member of the family that education seemed a luxury, hardly important in the daily struggle for survival. Indeed, Polish Americans who fought the uphill battle to educate themselves suffered ostracism by the community at large. As one Polish-American historian put it, "Members of Polonia feel bitter towards their educated class, resent its attitude, and consider it ungrateful."

Schooling for children seemed necessary only up to the age when they received Confirmation, which required a modicum of religious instruction. Toward this end, Polish Americans tried to establish Catholic schools within walking distance of their heavily populated neighborhoods. This proximity helped keep the group together, physically as well as culturally. Few Polish-American children attended public schools—

Students gather for a group portrait at the St. Joseph School in Meyersville, Texas.

their parents viewed them as "unchristian, pagan and demoralizing institutions" that would rob the children of their rich cultural heritage. As Joseph A. Wyrtrwal wrote in *Behold! The Polish Americans*, public school students

> don't hear any more about Poland, and if it is being referred to by the teachers it is usually with an air of superiority. The Polish heroes, except Kosciuszko and Pulaski, are not recognized, not worshipped in this country. America and not Poland is being constantly eulogized by the teachers and set as an example of national and spiritual superiority, and the Polish boy or girl soon does not know what to make of it. Has he not already a definite fatherland in Poland? Has he not learned to identify himself with Polish people which in the opinion of his father and mother are the best people in the world? How should he take the deprecatory remarks about his old country, and the light making or overlooking of his Polish heroes?

(continued on page 73)

TRADITION AND FAITH

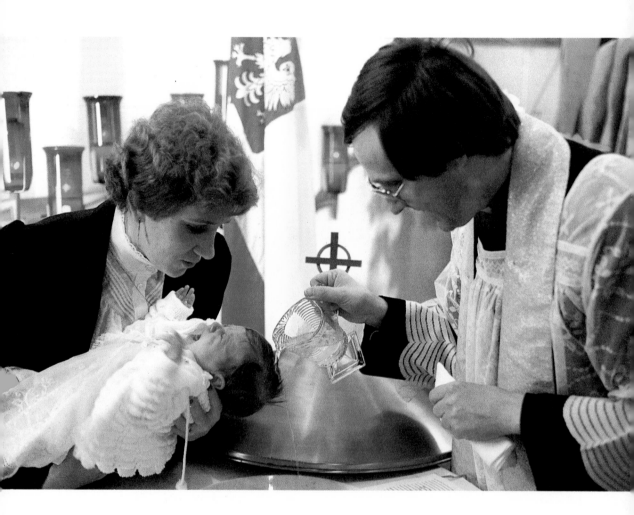

Many Polish Americans continue to honor the traditions and ceremonies of their religious heritage. The baptism rite welcomes a Polish-American infant (above) into the Polish Catholic community in Chicago. (Top right) In accordance with an Easter custom, a priest calls at the home of his parishioners to bless their food on the morning after Good Friday. (Lower right) Two Polish Americans visit a local church for a moment of private prayer.

Polish Americans' strong belief in freedom and democracy has fostered political activity designed to protect rights in the United States and to urge more freedoms in Poland. In Chicago, a Polish-American woman (top left) signs a petition circulated to end martial law in Poland. Spectators at a parade (lower left) cheer Illinois State Senator Judy Baar, a Polish American. (Above) During a Polish festival in Chicago, a lone pennant serves to remind a new generation of the ongoing struggle of the Solidarity party in Poland.

69

Fraternal organizations have combined with religious and political beliefs to help keep Polish culture and festivals such as this one (left) alive in the United States. Polish-American communities set up shops, clubs, and mutual aid societies that serve the community as well as perpetuate a sense of unity.

The 1970s saw a revival of ethnic pride and awareness: At the 1973 Pulaski Day Parade (above) in New York City, a Polish-American celebrates with a waving flag and a button that reads "Kiss Me I'm Polish."

(continued from page 64)

In 1918, when America entered World War I and antiforeign sentiment swept the nation, the federal government began to put pressure on the Polish schools to accept a standard curriculum and to use English, rather than Polish, as the first language.

Slavic children play on a slag heap, c. 1900.

Extreme Prejudice

In addition to the strain of everyday life, Polish Americans contended with another, sometimes more vexing, problem: prejudice. It seemed to be everywhere. Many of their neighbors viewed Poles as rowdy, disorganized, ignorant, filthy, and prone to drunkenness and sloth.

Corporate executive Edward J. Piszek has struggled to dignify the image of Polish Americans.

In the early 20th century, even President Woodrow Wilson, who had been a professor of law and economics at Princeton University, as well as the institution's president, publicly commented that Poles came from "the ranks where there was neither skill nor energy nor any initiative of quick intelligence." The impetus for these kinds of attack is unclear. Most cultures single out scapegoats to be the butt of unflattering jokes. The French take cheap shots at the Belgians and Irish Americans and Italian Americans trade frequent barbs, as do the English and the Scotch.

In any case, the stereotyping of Polish Americans has been reinforced by films, television, and plays. Perhaps the best-known fictional Polish American is Stanley Kowalski, the brutish character created by Tennessee Williams in his classic drama, *A Streetcar Named Desire*, first staged in 1948. For many Americans, Kowalski stood for all Polish Americans: violent, crude, poorly educated, and a heavy drinker. Since the late 1960s Polish—or "Polak"—jokes have enjoyed a great vogue. Many television comedians routinely tell jokes deprecating Poles, and these jokes gain momentum in the retelling. In the 1970s, television's "lovable bigot," Archie Bunker—the main character in the hit show "All in the Family"—reinforced prejudice against Polish Americans by calling his Polish-American son-in-law "meathead." Books like *It's Fun to Be a Polak* helped keep this prejudice alive. Even worse, Polish jokes have reached the highest levels of American society. When Ronald Reagan was running for president in 1980 he asked reporters, "How do you know who the Polish guy is at a cockfight?" He answered himself, "He's the one with the duck."

These "humorous" slights perpetuated the image of the "dumb Polak" by focusing on the lower-class backgrounds and peasant heritage of many Poles and fanning the flames of what some scholars perceive as an inferiority complex within the Polish-American community. To combat these attacks, in 1973 Edward J. Piszek, president of Mrs. Paul's Kitchens, a frozen-food manufacturer, launched a massive advertising campaign to stamp out Polish jokes. Working with the Orchard Lake Schools of Michigan, "Project Pole" was a half-million-dollar affair. It featured literate and intelligent ads, such as the one that showed a picture of celebrated novelist Joseph Conrad (1857–1924, née Jozef Korzeniowski) and read: "One of the greatest storytellers in the English language was a Pole. He changed his name, his language and the course of English literature." A lawsuit brought against the

American Broadcasting Company (ABC) by the Polish American Congress charged the network with refusing to allow equal airtime for a response to jokes viewed by many as "personal attacks on the character, intelligence, hygiene or appearance" of Americans of Polish descent. And Polish Americans took exception to an insulting skit on the "Carol Burnett Show," sending in bags of critical mail and forcing an apology on the air.

The issue of Polish stereotypes took a curious turn in November 1987, when a lengthy letter to the editor appeared in the *New York Times Book Review*. It was written by Stanislaus A. Blejwas, a Polish-American historian, and the subject of the letter was remarks made by another Polish American, Czeslaw Milosz, one of the leading Polish-language authors of the 20th century. Milosz, who had labored in obscurity for many years, rose to international celebrity in 1980, when he won the Nobel Prize for literature. He quickly became a source of enormous pride to the Polish-American community, which demanded his presence at a host of cultural events. But Milosz objected to acting as a spokesman for a community that had long neglected him. Indeed, the poet recently told an interviewer that he resents being invited to give public readings before "a lot of Poles, who come to see a famous Pole to lessen their own feeling of inferiority." Milosz went on to criticize the "incredible cultural crudeness" of many Polish Americans, a condition he traces to the "ghetto" mentality the community brought over from the homeland.

These opinions incensed Blejwas, who in his letter to the *Times* explained the feelings of Polish Americans in these words:

> After a decade of Polish jokes in the national media, jokes which even Mr. Milosz disliked, Polish-Americans took satisfaction in the recognition accorded to Mr. Milosz by the Nobel Prize, and we applauded him . . . . Like any other ethnic group [the Polish Americans] . . . have both good and negative points. Furthermore,

their diversity and socioeconomic and cultural integration into American society belies crude (there is that word again!) generalizations and stereotyping . . . . What are the . . . roots of the contempt of some Polish intellectuals for their Polish cousins? Is it due to a political culture still heavily encrusted with gentry contempt for those of lower social origin and rank? Is it simply the arrogance that many intellectuals, regardless of their national identity, felt for the masses? Or, in America, is it that sense of "alienation" our culture provokes which causes a writer of Mr. Milosz's obvious stature to stoop to the level of those who indulge themselves in Polish jokes?

Despite daily prejudice, Polish Americans frequently attended classes in order to prepare for the U.S. citizenship examination.

Polish and Proud

Despite the hostility of many other Americans, second-generation Polish Americans, as a group, have embraced the mainstream society of their country and tried to make their own place in it. The offspring of immigrants—as is the case with many groups—have rejected

Henry and Helen Gulczynski, a young Polish-American couple, proudly hold their baby daughter in 1947.

their parents' style of life and moved away from ethnic communities. As one Polish American put it:

> This generation of which I am a part, never had to face the problem of pulling away from Polonia. We had never properly belonged to it. To us it was a slowly decaying world of aged folks living largely in a dream. One day it would pass and there would remain only Americans whose forebears had once been Poles.

Yet subsequent generations have reversed the trend and rediscovered their origins. Indeed, the early 1970s saw a revival of awareness of Polish ethnicity; "Polish and Proud" bumper stickers adorned cars, and "Kiss Me I'm Polish" buttons abounded. The polka—a popular Polish dance—found new popularity; New Briton, Connecticut, boasts an annual "Polkabration."

Fraternal Organizations

The fraternal organizations and societies that the Poles created thrived and have played an important role in keeping Polish culture alive in America. The Polish National Alliance (PNA) was founded in 1880 in Philadelphia as the headquarters of a number of local societies that merged with the aim of promoting the restoration of an independent Poland. The Polish Roman Catholic Union (PRCU) had been created in 1873 and there were tensions between the two organizations. The PNA comprised mainly middle-class revolutionaries who wanted to unite Poland. They placed primary emphasis on the role of the state, rather than the church. The clergy and members of the PRCU felt more comfortable with the status quo.

Another group, the Polish Women's Alliance of America, worked toward the restoration of Poland as a part of the agenda of the international peace movement. In the calm before the First World War they proclaimed:

Poland today is like Lazarus, thrown on the bed of blood, fire and embers—murdering her own children by order of her enemies—sinking the steel in the breasts of her own sons, fathers and brothers . . . . In view of this terrible tax of blood, property and life devoured by war from our own unhappy nation, which is a crime of humanity and the world—we, the daughters of this downtrodden and blood bespattered unhappy country, do raise our mighty voice of mothers, daughters, sisters and wives suffering beyond measure, calling to all nations.

Strength in numbers was combined with a passionate belief in their cause. After nearly a decade of lobbying, in 1910 monuments to Polish heroes Pulaski and Kosciuszko were unveiled in the nation's capital on the 500th anniversary of the battle of Grunwald, when Poland defeated the horrific Teutonic Knights. And in 1937 Poles in New York City celebrated the anniversary of Pulaski's death with a glorious and joyful parade to honor the brave man, an activity that has been repeated every subsequent year. ∾

In 1925, Stephen Mizwa (top row, second from left) founded the Kosciuszko Foundation, an organization promoting cultural exchange between the United States and Poland.

CELEBRITIES AND CONTRIBUTIONS

In recent years, Polish Americans have entered every arena of the nation's life, and have done so in numbers and with talent. In baseball, for example—the most American of our national pastimes—Polish Americans have shone brilliantly. Stan Musial, born in Donors, Pennsylvania, in 1920, became one of the top stars in National League history. Known to St. Louis Cardinal fans as "Stan the Man," Musial won the Most Valuable Player award 3 times in a career that spanned 22 years, from 1941 to 1963. Elected to the Baseball Hall of Fame in 1969, he later served in the Cardinal's front office as a vice-president.

Another Polish-American star, Carl Yastrzemski, was born in 1939 on the east end of Long Island, New York, where his grandfather owned a potato farm. Yastrzemski joined the Boston Red Sox in 1961, replacing retired Red Sox great Ted Williams, the last man to bat over .400 for an entire season. "Yaz" proved a worthy successor, becoming one of the best all-around players of his era. In 1967 he won the triple crown—leading the American league in batting average, home runs, and runs batted in—while powering the Red Sox to the World Series. His long career ended in 1983.

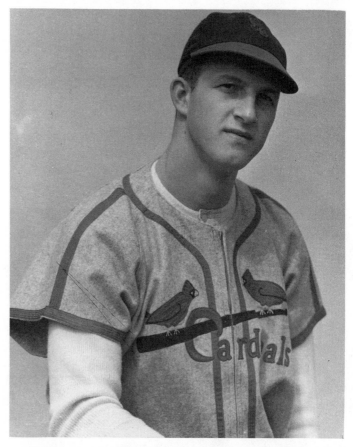

In 1942, Stan Musial, shown here at the St. Louis Cardinals' spring training camp, was known to reporters as baseball's "golden boy."

Other successful Polish-American ballplayers include Al Simmons, Tony Kubek, Greg "the Bull" Luzinski, Richie Zisk, Ted Kluszewski, Ed Lopat, Jim Konstanty, Ray Jablonski, Hank Majeski, George Shuba, Bill "Moose" Skowron, Ted Kazanski, Bob Kuzava, Cass Michaels, and Stan Lopata.

Poles in Entertainment

Poles have made great contributions to the screen, both the silver screen of Hollywood and the little screen of television. Pola Negri, Poland's first movie star, was born Appolonia Chalupec near the Polish town of Lipno in 1894. She made her debut in theater, then switched to the new medium of silent film, making her first appearance in a picture written and financed by herself, *Love and Passion* (1914). After starring in several more Polish films, she moved to Berlin and had a succession of hits, some directed by Ernst Lubitsch. He later went to Hollywood, as did Pola Negri, who became the first celluloid star to sign a contract with an American film company while working in Germany. In 1922 Negri arranged a meeting with the French tragedienne Sarah Bernhardt, at which she apologized for embarking on a Hollywood career at a time when movies were considered an inferior art to stage acting. The "divine Sarah" replied, "Don't be apologetic. I would have done the same thing but I was too early." In America, Negri's dark beauty won her many roles as a temptress—or *femme fatale*—in *Bella Donna*, *The Cheat*, *The Spanish Dancer*, and others. Much admired by film critics, Negri is ranked alongside such silent-movie stars as Greta Garbo and Gloria Swanson. She died in 1987.

Gloria Swanson, also of Polish descent, was born in about 1898 in Chicago, the daughter of a civilian employee of the U.S. Army who raised her on military bases throughout the continent. As a teenager living in Chicago, Swanson acted in small parts with the Essanay studio located there. In 1916 she married Wallace Beery, one of the most popular film actors of the silent era, and accompanied him to Hollywood. There she landed steady work in comedies, but longed for serious dramatic roles. They came her way in 1918, when she starred in *Society for Sale*, *Her Decision*, and several other films. She then caught the eye of director Cecil B. de Mille, who cast her in major hits such as *Don't Change Your Husband* (1919) and *Why Change Your Wife?* (1920).

In the 1920s Swanson became one of Hollywood's reigning goddesses, known for her temperamental behavior and exotic wardrobes. The bill for her bridal garb in *Her Love Story* (1924) was said to have been $100,000. In 1925 Swanson found a new husband—a French count—and seemed more glamorous than ever. Her salary rose to gigantic proportions, exceeding $20,000 per week at a time when corporation executives earned perhaps twice that much in a year. With the arrival of talkies in 1927, Swanson's career foundered, not because she lacked a strong speaking voice but because a new generation of leading ladies had stolen the spotlight. She made a triumphant return to the screen in 1950, when she played aging movie star Norma Desmond in *Sunset Boulevard*.

Two of the most distinguished Polish-American film artists seldom appeared before the public. Joseph L. Mankiewicz, born in 1909, was a producer, director,

Carl Yastrzemski was one of the few baseball players to collect 3,000 hits in a career.

and scriptwriter who began his career as a journalist. His talent as a writer led him to Hollywood, where he produced such classics as *The Philadelphia Story* (1940) and *Woman of the Year* (1942), both starring Katharine Hepburn. In 1950 he directed *All About Eve*, which won the Academy Award for Best Picture and scored triumphs for Mankiewicz and star Bette Davis. Mankiewicz's brother Herman (1898–1953) also started his career in newspapers. He then went to Hollywood and wrote scripts, mostly comedies. In 1941, he won an Oscar for his screenplay for *Citizen Kane*, often called one of the best movies of all time. A celebrated wit, Mankiewicz made a remark about Orson Welles, *Citizen Kane*'s brilliant star and director, that later became film lore and is listed in *Bartlett's Familiar Quotations*. As Welles strolled through the set one day, enveloped in his own egotism, Mankiewicz muttered, "There but for the grace of God goes God."

A later generation of Polish filmmakers has earned a large reputation in the international film community. Roman Polanski, born in Paris in 1933, moved to Poland with his parents when he was three years old. When the Nazis invaded Poland, Polanski's Jewish parents were both sent to a concentration camp, and their son hid with several different Polish families. In 1962 he directed his first film—the only one he ever made in Poland—*Knife in the Water*, which received great critical acclaim. Polanski then moved to Britain, where he made three films. One of them, *Dance of the Vampires* (1967), featured American actress Sharon Tate, who became his wife. Polanski then set out for Hollywood, and in 1968 made the thriller *Rosemary's Baby*. It starred Mia Farrow and was a huge popular success. On August 8, 1968, Sharon Tate and others staying in Polanski's Bel Air villa died at the hands of members of mass-murderer Charles Manson's cult. Although he was devastated by this catastrophe, Polanski eventually went on to direct other films, including *Tess*, in 1980, starring Nastassia Kinski.

Poland's most prominent contemporary filmmaker today is Andrzej Wajda. The films Wajda has made in Poland receive critical praise all over the world, though his themes—which probe sensitive areas of the Polish conscience—have incensed many of his compatriots. His film *Danton*, about the French Revolution, has been called an allegory of events occurring in Poland following the Solidarity strike. Another recent Wajda film, *A Love in Germany*, is a portrayal of the bureaucracy of the Nazi regime. Both these later films were shot in France.

Screen siren Pola Negri is widely credited with introducing the fashion of painted toenails to American women.

In 1928, Gloria Swanson sits beside director Raoul Walsh during the filming of Sadie Thompson.

Polish music has been brought to the American public by a number of popular singers, among them Bobby Vinton, "the Polish Prince." His huge hit in 1974, "My Melody of Love," was based on a Polish folk song and is sung partly in Polish. Vinton's other hits include "Roses are Red," "Blue on Blue," and "Blue Velvet." The entertainer had his own television show in the 1970s, and enjoys extreme popularity among the Polish-American areas of the Midwest. Many of his songs are Polish, and he has even made an album that consists entirely of polkas.

Liberace, the flamboyant pianist and showman who died in 1987 of acquired immune deficiency syndrome (AIDS), also brought Polish music, including polkas, to American audiences. A virtuoso pianist who might have flourished on the classical concert stage, Liberace chose instead to popularize the music he loved with elaborate shows, outrageous costumes, and his trademark candelabra perched atop a grand piano.

Poles as Pols

No recent Polish American has had a more illustrious career in politics than Edmund Muskie. Born in 1914 to Polish immigrants living in Rumford, Maine, Muskie began his career as a lawyer. After serving in the navy during World War II, he won election to the Maine legislature. In 1955 he became the state's first Polish-American governor and also broke an 18-year Republican monopoly on the office. Three years later he achieved another first, becoming the first Polish American to win a seat in the U.S. Senate. He won reelection in 1964, and in 1968 Muskie became the Democratic party's vice-presidential candidate on a ticket headed by Hubert H. Humphrey. The team lost a close contest to Republicans Richard M. Nixon and Spiro T. Agnew. Muskie reclaimed his Senate seat in 1970. In the next election year, 1972, he emerged as the top contender for the party's presidential nomination, but his campaign ran aground. A year later, when the Watergate scandal beset the Nixon administration, congressional hearings unearthed evidence that Muskie's bid had been sabotaged by operatives working for the Republican Committee to Reelect the President. In 1979, Muskie resigned his post in the Senate to accept an emergency appointment as secretary of state, helping shore up the ailing administration of President Jimmy Carter. Thereafter Muskie retired from politics, but resurfaced in 1986, when President Ronald Reagan appointed him to the Tower Commission, a three-man panel of distinguished public servants charged with reviewing the Iran-Contra affair.

Another Polish American also held high office during the Carter administration: National Security Ad-

Roman Polanski consults with his cinematographer on the set of The Tenant, *filmed in Paris in 1975.*

visor Zbigniew Brzezinski. Born in Poland in 1928, he became disenchanted with the country's Communist regime and in 1958 immigrated to the United States. He taught government at Harvard University, and was on the faculty of Columbia University when Carter appointed him to the National Security Council (NSC) in 1976. In that post he often feuded with Secretary of State Cyrus Vance, who advocated a less combative stance toward the Soviet Union. But Brzezinski and

Vance worked together to assist Carter during his greatest presidential triumph: the Camp David peace accord signed in 1979 by Israel's premier Menachem Begin and Egyptian president Anwar Sadat. After Carter lost his reelection bid in 1980, Brzezinski joined Georgetown University's Center for Strategic International Studies.

Barbara Milkulski, a Democratic representative from Maryland, has helped rekindle Polish-American pride. She has argued for an integrated approach to ethnicity:

> Because of old prejudices and new fears, anger is generated against other minority groups rather than

In 1972, U.S. senator Edmund Muskie displays a bumper sticker bearing his original Polish name.

those who have power. What is needed is an alliance of white and black; white collar, blue collar, and no collar based upon mutual need, interdependence and respect, an alliance to develop . . . a new kind of community organization and political participation.

Polish-American Dan Rostenkowski, a Chicago Democrat, held a crucial post during the Republican era dominated by President Ronald Reagan. As chairman of the House Ways and Means Committee, Rostenkowski was largely responsible for writing the tax reform bill of 1987.

Polish Americans have long composed a large segment of the working community, and some members of the group have risen to high positions within the ranks of organized labor. Joseph "Jock" Yablonski, the United Mine Workers' insurgent candidate for union president in 1969, embodied the organization's growing reformist beliefs. When Yablonski lost his campaign for UMW president in a disputed election, he filed a complaint with the U.S. Department of Labor, alleging some 100 election violations. He then threatened to sue the incumbent president, Tony Boyle. But the trial never occurred: On New Year's Eve, 1970, Yablonski, his wife Margaret, and their daughter Charlotte were shot to death by three hired gunmen. Boyle was later jailed for Yablonski's death.

Poets and Writers, Rebels and Intellectuals

During the 1950s a number of discontented intellectuals left Poland to make their home in North America. Among them was Jerzy Kosinski. Born in 1933, Kosinski grew up in Russia, then came to the United States in 1957. He studied at Columbia University and applied himself to mastering English. Under the pseudonym Joseph Novak, Kosinski wrote two nonfiction accounts of the Soviet Union, *The Future is Ours, Comrade* (1960) and *No Third Path* (1962). His first novel, *The Painted*

Former National Security Adviser Zbigniew Brzezinski is the author of The Soviet Bloc, *a standard political science text.*

Bird, published in 1965, describes the experiences of a young boy adrift in the Polish war zone during World War II. The novel's vivid depiction of war impressed critics, and Kosinski's next novel, *Steps*, was chosen the National Book Award winner in 1968. Kosinski's short novel, *Being There* (1973), about an innocent gardener who bungles his way to the presidency, became a highly successful film starring Peter Sellers. Kosinski was the first foreign-born and -educated writer elected president of the American branch of the worldwide organization, Poets, Essayists, and Novelists (PEN). He has taught at Yale University.

Polish émigré Czeslaw Milosz was born in Lithuania in 1911, but received his education in Poland. After World War II he entered the country's diplomatic corps. Stationed in Paris from 1945–50, he pursued a career as a writer, gaining a reputation in Europe for his poetry and prose. He came to the attention of American readers in 1953, with the English translation of *The Captive Mind*, a meditation on the plight of Polish writers forced to live under a communist regime. In 1960 he immigrated to the United States and accepted a teaching job at the University of California. Ten years later, Milosz was naturalized, and 10 years after that he won the Noble Prize for literature. His poetry, collected in *Selected Poems* (1972), *Bells in Winter* (1978), and other volumes, mingles lyrical imagery with penetrating insight. An accomplished prose writer, Milosz wrote an autobiographical novel, *The Issa Valley* (1981), which beautifully evokes the landscape of his youth.

A third Polish-American writer, Isaac Bashevis Singer, writes in Yiddish, the language spoken by much of the world's Jewish population. Born in Poland in 1904, Singer disappointed his parents by choosing to become a writer, rather than a rabbi, following in the footsteps of his older brother, Israel Joshua Singer, also a novelist. Both immigrated to New York City in the 1930s and wrote fiction published in the *Jewish Daily*

Forward. As I. B. Singer's reputation grew, a cry went up for English versions of his work, and translations began to appear—of *The Family Moskat* (1950), *Satan in Goray* (1955), and *The Magician of Lublin* (1960). These novels proved popular, but Singer won even more followers with his short stories, fables about the ghetto life of Polish Jews, including "Gimpel the Fool" (1957) and "The Spinoza of Market Street" (1961). Forty-seven of Singer's short tales were gathered in *Collected Stories,* published in 1982, four years after Singer won the Nobel Prize for literature. Singer has written children's stories and also memoirs, including *Lost in America* (1981), a reminiscence of his life in the New World.

In 1983, U.S. representative Barbara Mikulski called for the resignation of Defense Secretary Caspar Weinberger.

Another Polish American enriched the intellectual life of his adopted country in a different way. Stephen Mizwa immigrated to the United States in 1910. He worked at a variety of jobs—primarily as a manual laborer—before pursuing an advanced education. He graduated from Amherst College, then earned a master's degree from Harvard. Mizwa became a teacher and in 1925 founded the Kosciuszko Foundation in New York City with the help of the president of Vassar College, Henry Noble MacCracken, and Samuel M. Vauvlain, president of Baldwin Locomotive Works. The organization supports serious scholarship in Polish studies and encourages Polish-American youths to pursue intellectual achievement. The Kosciuszko Foundation's specific goals include:

Czeslaw Milosz (left) received the Nobel Prize for literature from Sweden's King Karl Gustaf in 1980.

1. To grant voluntary financial aid to deserving Polish students desiring to study at institutions of higher learning in the United States of America; and to deserving American students hoping to study in Poland.

2. To encourage and aid the exchange of professors, scholars, and lecturers between Poland and the United States of America.

3. To cultivate closer intellectual and cultural relations between Poland and the United States in such ways and by which means as may from time to time seem wise, in the judgement of the Board of Directors of the Corporation.

The foundation subsidizes publication of works on Poland—including a number of doctoral dissertations—poetry readings, exhibits, concerts, and other cultural events. Since World War II, the organization has emphasized aiding refugee scholars from Poland.

The contributions of Polish Americans are too many and too varied to sum up easily. Americans of Polish descent have entered into and become important in just about every aspect of American life. In the words of W.S. Kuniczak, a notable Polish-American novelist:

There have been no significant movements in American history in which the Poles have not played a part, no area of American life in which they have not left an imprint of their own. They are a vital and energetic community of Americans, of many talents and considerable material resources, whose voice is only now beginning to be heard. ∾

Isaac Bashevis Singer recounted his Polish childhood in his memoir In My Father's Court.

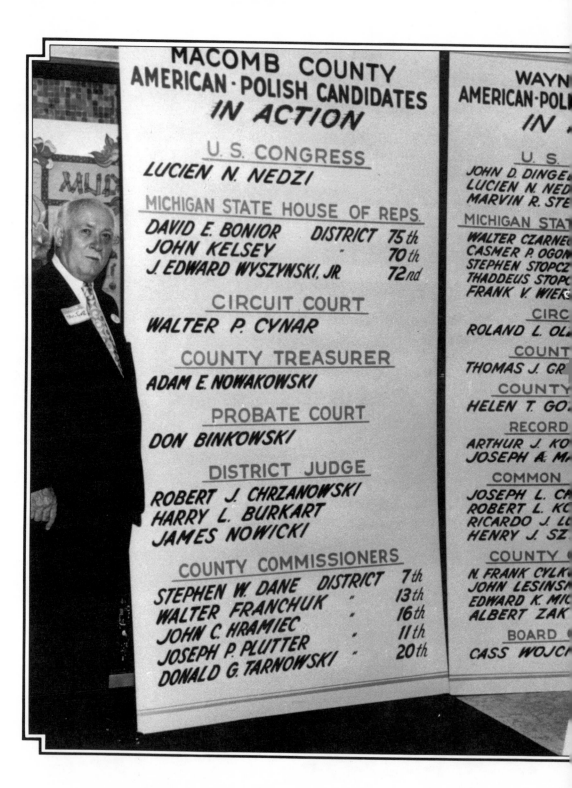

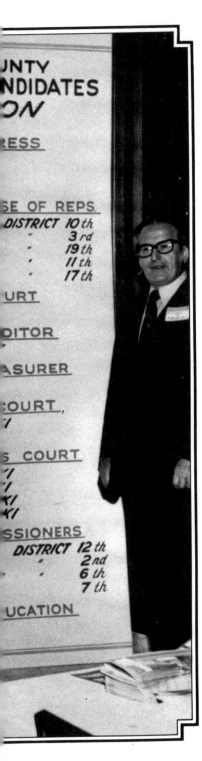

Michigan's Polish Action Council charts Polish Americans in politics.

THE VOICE OF POLONIA

A recently published history of Polish Americans by John Bukowczyk takes its title, *And My Children Did Not Know Me*, from a line in a Polish folk song whose lyrics lament the experience of too many Polish Americans:

When I journeyed from America . . .
And the foundry where I labored,
In pray'r my hands thanked our Father,
Hands that never shirked their labor.
Soon I came to New York City,
To the agent for my passage.
And the agents asked me if I
Had three hundred dollars with me.
"Ask me not such foolish questions.
For I carry gold and silver."
When I crossed the ocean midway,
No land could I see, sweet Virgin.
Our ship's captain was right busy,
Seeing, cheering all the people.
When I laid my eyes on Hamburg,
I thought I saw God Almighty.
When at last I landed safely,
"Lord," I prayed, "I thank thee for this.
O how grateful am I, dear God,
that I've crossed the ocean safely."
Berlin came next after Hamburg,

Members of the Alliance College faculty gather for a special convocation in 1972.

"Barmaid, I will have some good wine."
Then I left Berlin for Krakow;
There my wife was waiting for me.
And my children did not know me,
For they fled from me, a stranger.
"My dear children, I'm your papa;
Three long years I have not seen you."

Remembering and Forgetting

A century ago, Poles who journeyed to America to start new lives worried about the curse of forgetfulness. They especially feared that their offspring would lose touch with the heritage of the homeland. Bukowcyz's study quotes a letter written by a concerned immigrant sometime between 1876 and 1878:

> But what about the second, third and fourth generations? What of the children born of German, Irish, or American mothers? Sooner or later they will forget. They will change everything, even their names, which English teeth find too difficult to chew and which interfere with business. How long this will take is difficult to say. But just as Poland disappeared, so will this same sad fate inevitably befall her children who, today, are scattered throughout the world.

The author of this letter, Henryk Sienkiewicz, probably need not have fretted, for once the children of the original immigrants felt secure in American society, they tended to cling tenaciously to their heritage—even in the face of extreme prejudice.

Though not all immigrants went home to Poland, many retained tangible connections with the Old World, generally through friends or relatives still living in the old country. Often those who forsook Poland felt responsible for the well-being of those they left behind. Even today, the grandchildren of immigrants—people who think of themselves as American rather than Polish—send clothing and money to relatives they have never met. One third-generation Polish-American woman mails "home" old clothing carefully lined with American cash—5- and 10-dollar bills that probably would be confiscated if the Communist authorities discovered them.

Bukowcyz also quotes an excerpt from "Why I Am Proud of My Polish Ancestry," an essay that won an award in a contest sponsored by *Reader's Digest* in the 1950s. At one point the essayist wrote:

Members of the Polish American Congress protest Poland's Communist regime on the 30th anniversary of the Polish People's Republic.

I am proud that I am a Pole—and for good reasons. My Polish ancestry entitles me to share in a history that is rich in God-fearing heroes and heroines, who have championed the cause of liberty, peace, and freedom; of honesty and justice; of equality and brotherhood. Polish descent offers a heritage of honor . . . YES, I am proud I am a Pole—for a good Pole has every right and reason to be a good American.

As much as Polish Americans have sought to hold on to the past, they realize that the old methods for keeping alive their heritage no longer suffice. For example, on June 30, 1987, Alliance College in Cambridge Springs, Pennsylvania, closed its doors. Founded in 1912, Alliance had been the only remaining American college to specialize in Polish culture; the college was sponsored by the Polish National Alliance. Despite its venerable history and valuable role, the institution had

Playwright Janusz Glowacki is one of many Polish émigrés who have enriched the cultural life of the United States.

fallen sadly into debt and mismanagement and had trouble recruiting students.

This development echoes the fears expressed in 1903 by George Brandes, a Polish American quoted in Joseph A. Wyrtrwal's *Behold! The Polish Americans:*

> The fear of losing the children haunts the older generation. It is not merely the natural desire of parent to retain influence over the child. Nor is it simply the dread that the wayward offspring will mar the good name of the immigrant group by abuse of his newly found freedom. It is a vague uneasiness that a delicate network of precious traditions is being ruthlessly torn asunder, that a whole world of ideals is crashing into ruins; and amidst this desolation the fathers and mothers picture themselves wandering about lonely in vain search of their lost children.

Polish Americans are not the only ethnic group that faces this dilemma. As Italian Americans, Irish Americans, Jewish Americans, and other minorities have made headway in their efforts to enter the larger, surrounding culture, they have paid a price. And acceptance into the mainstream has not been complete. As Congresswoman Barbara Milkulski has put it, America, rather than being a melting pot, seems

> a sizzling cauldron for the ethnic American who feels that he has been politically extorted by both government and private enterprise. The ethnic American is sick of being stereotyped as a racist and dullard by phony white liberals, pseudo-black militants and patronizing bureaucrats. He pays the bill for every major government program and gets nothing or little in the way of return. Tricked by the rhetoric of the illusionary funding for black-oriented social programs, he turns his anger to race—when he himself is the victim of class prejudice. He has worked hard . . . to become a "good American"; he and his sons have fought on every battlefield—then he is made fun of because he likes the flag.

Polish filmmaker Zbigniew Rybczynski won an Academy Award for best animated short subject for his film Tango *in 1983.*

In 1973, students from Polish-language schools marched in the Pulaski Day parade in New York City.

Immigrants and Exiles

To some extent renewed ethnic vigor in the Polish-American community stems from the most recent wave of Polish immigrants. Many arrived after World War II and were admitted to the United States by the Special Displaced Persons Act of 1948 and subsequent laws intended to aid refugees. Unlike the first wave of immigrants, these newcomers had suffered the effects of world war. Some had spent five to six years in work camps or prisons in Germany or Russia; others had fought with the Allied armies in Europe or wandered homeless after being deported by the Soviets, who had made Poland a satellite of their own communist country. The numbers of immigrants rose in the 1980s, after General Jaruzelski tightened restrictions. Most of these new immigrants came from the cities and had been involved in a variety of occupations.

Some of these immigrants, members of Poland's intelligentsia, feel stifled by the repressions of the Soviet regime. In the United States they often congregate in cultural communities alongside artists and other exiles seeking greater freedom. One such émigré, New Yorker

Janusz Glowacki, received critical acclaim for his play *Hunting Cockroaches*, which concerns the immigrant experience. Glowacki told the *New York Times* that waiting for reviews in Poland is different from waiting for them here. In Poland a good review in the official paper (distrusted by intellectuals) could mean no one would show up to see the play. "But a very bad review in the official press could cause a line in front of the theatre the very next day."

Another recent immigrant is filmmaker Zbibniew Rybcyznski, whose remarkable short film *Tango* (made in Poland) won an Oscar. His films, generally shorts and usually animated, masterfully portray the repetitiveness and constraints of life in a repressive society. Rybcyznski made numerous films in Poland—he was given the money and the equipment to do so in order to fulfill the government-owned studio's quota—but his best films have been banned in his homeland. In 1987 he was at work on music videos and a movie with Glowacki about the adventures of the son of Citizen Kane, a character invented by an earlier Polish American, Herman Mankiewicz.

The Old System

Despite these changes, some Poles still venture to North America for the same reason their forebears did a century ago: to make money quickly and then return home. One such immigrant, Witold Wroblewski, met a fate that sums up the conflicting sides of the American experience. In 1986 he arrived in New York City with the intention of earning enough money to pay for an operation needed by his paralyzed son. Wroblewski had been working for eight months at a gas station in Riverdale, Long Island, when robbers held up the place. They shot at a glass door, and fragments of it and bullets were sent into Wroblewski's face. Luckily, he survived, and his wife and ailing son were able to join him in the United States. Concerned New Yorkers raised

$80,000 for the operation that will help 7-year-old Wojtek Wroblewski walk again.

An Old-Style Neighborhood

As late as 1987, a large community of Polish immigrants lived in Greenpoint, a neighborhood in the New York City borough of Brooklyn. Its main thoroughfare, Manhattan Avenue, seems transported from Warsaw or Kraków. The employees in the supermarket still converse in Polish and many small shops have hand-lettered signs written in Polish. Clothiers selling Polish furs—hats and coats—nestle up against travel agencies offering discount plane tickets to the homeland. Wedding parties often celebrate at the local community center, then feast at one of the nearby ethnic restaurants, which specialize in treats such as pickled herring, stuffed derma, and *kielbasa*—Polish sausage. The neighborhood's Catholic churches include large stone structures built of gray stone and smaller buildings built of clapboard glossed with shiny white paint.

Many of Greenpoint's Polish Americans live on the quiet streets that empty into or parallel Manhattan Avenue. Here two- and three-story apartment buildings—erected a century ago as single-family dwellings—sport new exteriors made of composition shingle or aluminum siding. Today these apartments accommodate several families who inhabit "railroad" or "dumbbell" apartments—long narrow flats broken up into connecting rooms that afford no privacy and little light. Many of the apartments serve as a sort of dormitory for single men—usually immigrants just arrived from Poland and too poor to rent entire apartments for themselves. These immigrants pay a monthly fee for sleeping space—a cot crammed alongside several others. In the building's foyer a visitor will sometimes see six or seven different names taped to a mailbox meant to serve a single family.

Greenpoint attracts so many Polish immigrants because the existing community helps them adjust to life

The G train carries Polish Americans from their neighborhood in Greenpoint, Brooklyn, to the wider world of metropolitan New York.

in the United States. Jobs often await men in a nearby glass factory, and many women ride the subway to Manhattan where they work in the evenings cleaning large office buildings. On Saturday night, newcomers join more established Polish Americans in the neighborhood's eateries and pubs or convene for political discussions in the local outpost of Solidarity. On Sundays, Polish Americans of different generations, clad in suits and fine dresses, fill the pews of Greenpoint's churches.

Recent events have caused many Polish Americans to renew their ties with Poland. The story of Solidarity reminds Polish Americans of their connection to an ancestral homeland; it also reminds them that they are lucky to have found a nation that has granted them the opportunity denied them in Poland. In the years to come Poles will undoubtedly continue to view the United States as a haven of freedom and democracy, just as they did two centuries ago. In the future, more Poles will probably leave behind a familiar life for the possibilities offered by America, and they will enrich an ethnic community that has already made a lasting mark on the larger society that contains it. ✍

FURTHER READING

Bukowczyk, John J. *And My Children Did Not Know Me: A History of the Polish-Americans.* Bloomington, IN: Indiana University Press, 1987.

Davies, Norman. *Heart of Europe: A Short History of Poland.* New York: Oxford University Press, 1986.

Kuniczak, W. S. *My Name Is Million: An Illustrated History of the Poles in America.* New York: Doubleday, 1978.

Mocha, Frank, ed. *Poles in America: Bicentennial Essays.* Stevens Point, WI: Worzalla Publishing Co., 1978.

Renkiewicz, Frank. *The Poles in America 1608–1972: A Chronology and Fact Book.* Dobbs Ferry, NY: Oceana Publications Inc., 1973.

Tec, Nechama. *Dry Tears.* New York: Oxford University Press, 1985.

———. *When Light Pierced the Darkness: Righteous Christians and the Polish Jews.* New York: Oxford University Press, 1986.

Thomas, William I., and Florian Znaniecki. *The Polish Peasant in Europe and America.* Volume II. New York: Dover, 1958.

Wrobel, Paul. *Our Way: Family, Parish, and Neighborhood in a Polish-American Community.* Notre Dame, Indiana: University of Notre Dame Press, 1979.

Wyrtrwal, Joseph A. *Behold! The Polish Americans.* Detroit: Endurance Press, 1977.

INDEX

PICTURE CREDITS

We would like to thank the following sources for providing photographs: AP/ Wide World Photos: pp. 36, 65, 94, 101; Arizona Historical Foundation: p. 45; J. Berrdt: p. 16; The Bettmann Archive: pp. 22, 32, 33, 39, 49, 95; British Museum: p. 27; Courtesy of Karyn Browne: p. 78; Chicago Historical Society: p. 14; Click, Chicago: pp. 68 (bottom), 70; Foto Marburg/Art Resource: pp. 20, 21; Robert Frerck/Click, Chicago: p. 71 (top); Lewis W. Hine/International Museum of Photography at George Eastman House: pp. 57, 62; Illinois Labor History Society: pp. 52–53; Immigration History Research Center, University of Minnesota; Institute of Texan Cultures: pp. 54, 73; Gary Irving/Click, Chicago: p. 69; Kosciuszko Foundation: pp. 12–13, 80, 96; Mitchell Lewandowski/Kosciuszko Foundation: p. 99; Library of Congress: pp. 15, 29, 31, 34, 41, 42, 46, 55, 73, 86; National Archives: pp. 35, 50; New York Public Library: pp. 18–19, 25, 58; Ontario Archives: p. 43; PAR/NYC: pp. 56, 105; Marc Pokempner/Click, Chicago: pp. 67 (bottom), 68 (top); Sy Rubin/Kosciuszko Foundation: p. 102; Brian Seed/Click, Chicago: pp. 66, 71 (bottom); Martha Swope: p. 100; Katrina Thomas: pp. 67 (top), 72; UPI/Bettmann Newsphotos: pp. 61, 82, 84, 87, 89, 90, 92, 93; VeCellio: p. 23; Western Reserve Historical Society: p. 77; Westminster Magazine, 1774: p. 28; Wojcieck Fabjaniak/Kosciuszko Foundation: p. 74; Yerkes Observatory: p. 24

RACHEL TOOR received a degree in English from Yale University and is currently an editor at a major publishing house in New York City. She lives in Brooklyn, New York, and this is her first book.

DANIEL PATRICK MOYNIHAN is the senior United States senator from New York. He is also the only person in American history to serve in the cabinets or subcabinets of four successive presidents—Kennedy, Johnson, Nixon, and Ford. Formerly a professor of government at Harvard University, he has written and edited many books, including *Beyond the Melting Pot, Ethnicity: Theory and Experience* (both with Nathan Glazer), *Loyalties,* and *Family and Nation.*